...guage Teaching

Teaching and
Learning Grammar

Jeremy Harmer

Longman

London   New York

Longman Group UK Limited
Longman House, Burnt Mill
Harlow, Essex CM20 2JE, England
and Associated Companies throughout the world.

Distributed in the United States of America
by Longman Publishing, New York

First published 1987
Ninth impression 1993

British Library Cataloguing in Publication Data
Harmer, Jeremy, *1947–*
   Teaching and learning grammar. –
   (Longman keys to language teaching).
   1. English language–Study and teaching
   –Foreign speakers
   I. Title
   428.2   PE1128

ISBN 0-582-74623-X

Library of Congress Cataloguing in Publication Data
Harmer, Jeremy.
   Teaching and learning grammar.
   (Longman keys to language teaching)
   Bibliography p. 69
   1. Language and languages – Study and teaching.
2. Grammar, Comparative and general – Study and
teaching.   I. Title   II. Series.
P53.H366   1987   418'.007   87-3954
ISBN 0-582-74623-X

Typeset in Monophoto Century Schoolbook by
Vision Typesetting, Manchester

Printed in Malaysia by CL

We are grateful to the following for permission to
reproduce copyright photographs:

Bruce Coleman Limited for page 31 (middle); John
Topham Picture Library for page 31 (bottom);
Picturepoint Limited for page 31 (top).

Author's note

I would like to record my thanks for the stimulating and helpful comments made by the editor of the *Keys* series, Neville Grant, as this book has evolved.

Teaching and Learning Grammar is dedicated to the memory of Walter Plumb, in the hope that he would have approved.

Jeremy Harmer.
Cambridge, UK.
November 1986

Contents

Preface

FOR SOME TIME, many teachers have felt the need for a series of handbooks designed for ordinary teachers in ordinary classrooms. So many books these days seem to be written for privileged teachers in privileged environments – teachers with large classrooms, large budgets for expensive equipment, and small classes!

Most of us are not so lucky: most ordinary teachers are short of almost everything except students. They don't have a lot of time for elaborate theories, time-consuming classroom routines, and complicated jargon.

Longman Keys to Language Teaching have been written especially for the ordinary teacher. The books offer sound, practical, down-to-earth advice on basic techniques and approaches in the classroom. Most of the suggested activities can be adapted and used for almost any class, by any teacher.

In *Teaching and Learning Grammar*, Jeremy Harmer deals with one of the most controversial questions in ELT – should we teach grammar? If so, when, and how? There was a time when 'Doctor Grammar' was seen as a cure for everything. Later, Dr Grammar became a cure worse than any disease! This book provides a very useful over-view of the various approaches and techniques that teachers can use in teaching grammar in their classrooms. The book contains many valuable classroom examples of teaching grammar in action.

Neville Grant

Introduction

What is grammar?

The *Longman Dictionary of Contemporary English* defines grammar as '(The study and practice of) the rules by which words change their forms and are combined into sentences'. There are two basic elements in this definition: the rules of grammar; and the study and practice of the rules.

The rules of grammar, as the dictionary suggests, are about how words change and how they are put together into sentences. For example, our knowledge of grammar tells us that the word *walk* changes to *walked* in the past tense. This is an example of a word changing its form.

Our knowledge of grammar will also tell us what to do if we want to put the phrase *not many* into the sentence *There are oranges on the shelf* (There are not many oranges on the shelf). This is an example of how words are combined into sentences.

Grammar, then, is the way in which words change themselves and group together to make sentences. The grammar of a language is what happens to words when they become plural or negative, or what word order is used when we make questions or join two clauses to make one sentence. This is the grammar that we will be considering in this book.

How will grammar be dealt with in this book?

In this book we will be looking at the ways in which students can learn and acquire a working knowledge of the English grammatical system. We will look at various different ideas for introducing this knowledge, how to practise it, how to make it enjoyable, how to get students to think about grammatical areas and how to test it.

Returning to our dictionary definition we can say that *Teaching and Learning Grammar* focuses on the *practice* rather than the *study* of grammar.

Exercises

1 What does 'grammar' mean to you?
2 Try to remember when you last studied 'grammar': what did you do in the classroom?
3 What grammatical rules or knowledge have you learnt about any language (including your own)?

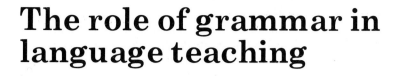

The role of grammar in language teaching

Task: Before you read this chapter, decide which of the following statements you agree with:
1 Students need to be given details of grammar rules if they are to learn English successfully.
2 Children do not learn grammar rules when they acquire their first language, so adults don't need to either.
3 If students get enough chance to practise using a language, they don't need to learn grammar.
4 It is helpful for students to be aware of grammatical information about the language.
5 Making students aware of grammatical facts is one of the things a teacher can do, but there are many other activities in the classroom which are just as important – like reading, listening, and fluency activities.

We are going to look at a number of techniques for presenting and practising grammar in the following chapters. In some of these activities the grammatical information we give the students will be extremely *covert* and in some cases grammatical information will be made extremely *overt*. What is the difference between these two concepts?

Covert and overt

Covert grammar teaching is where grammatical facts are hidden from the students – even though they are learning the language. In other words, the students may be asked to do an information gap activity (see page 44) or read a text (see page 35) where new grammar is practised or introduced, but their attention will be drawn to the activity or to the text and *not* to the grammar. With covert grammar, teachers help the students to acquire and/or practise the language, but they do not draw conscious attention to any of the grammatical facts of the language.

Overt grammar teaching means that the teacher actually provides the students with grammatical rules and explanations – the information is openly presented, in other words. Some techniques for the presentation of new language – for example where the teacher explains how present simple questions need *do* or *does* – are extremely overt: in chapter four we will look at many problem-solving and discovery exercises that encourage the students to consider grammatical information in some detail – and which we would therefore call overt.

So, with overt teaching we are explicit and open about the grammar of the language, but with covert teaching we simply get students to work with new language and hope that they will more or less subconsciously absorb grammatical information which will help them to acquire the language as a whole.

Which kind of grammar teaching is best? Should we just practise using the language and hope that the grammar 'rubs off' on the students? Or should we practise using the language and also from time to time draw students' attention to the language's formal grammatical characteristics? Should we teach grammar at all?

Grammar-less teaching?

In recent years the emphasis has shifted away from the teaching of grammar. Teachers have concentrated on other issues, such as how people learn languages and what they want to say. Many teachers and writers discussed these questions and gradually created a new way of looking at teaching called the *communicative approach*. Two of the main issues in the communicative approach were the teaching of *language functions*, and the use of *communicative activities*. Together with these issues, a distinction has been made between *acquisition* and *learning*.

Language functions

Some people felt that teaching the grammar of the language did not necessarily help people to use the language. Just because, for example, somebody knew the verb *to be*, it did not mean that he or she would be able to use it to introduce themselves or others. Language is used, the argument went, actually to *do* things, to perform certain functions, like inviting, apologising, introducing, suggesting, expressing likes, and so on. Instead of teaching grammar, we should teach functions.

The problem, of course, is that the sentences that perform functions are made up of grammatical elements. Even the simple introduction 'I'm John and this is Mary' is made up of the grammatical elements the verb *to be* and a demonstrative pronoun. Courses based only on teaching functions (at beginner and elementary levels) run into the problem that students have to know grammar to perform the functions – but grammar is often not being taught.

There is now a general feeling that students do need to learn how to perform the functions of language, but that they need a grammatical base as well. Modern courses often teach a grammatical structure and then get students to use it as part of a functional conversation. An example of this would be the students learning the *going to* future. They might first learn how to ask simple questions using the new structure ('What are you going to do for your holidays?'). Later the new structure can be incorporated into a functional exchange, for example:

A: Where are you off to?
B: I'm going to walk to the shops.
A: You'd better take an umbrella!
B: Why?
A: It's going to rain.

Communicative activities

One of the main effects of the communicative approach has been the realisation that just getting students to perform drills or engage in controlled practice may not be enough to help them to stand on their own feet as users of English. Other types of activity are needed where students can talk (or write) freely and use all or any of the language that they know. In other words, there must be occasions when students in the classroom use language to communicate ideas, not just to practise language. There are now many books about activities like role playing, problem-solving, discussions, games, and project work which encourage students to communicate.

Communicative activities have many advantages: they are usually enjoyable; they give students a chance to use their language; they allow both students and teachers to see how well the students are doing in their language learning; and they give a break from the normal teacher–students arrangement in a classroom.

The question is, of course, how much they should be used. Some people have argued that all English teaching should only be concerned with activities like this. Most teachers, however, say that activities like this should form only a part of the students' timetable.

Acquisition and learning

All children seem to acquire language without being taught it. It appears that they hear lots of language, and in a subconscious way – without thinking about it – they gradually pick it up until they can use their native language efficiently. People who go and live in another country and pick up the language without actually going to language classes, presumably acquire their ability to use the language in the same way, to some extent. Maybe, then, we don't need to 'teach' language at all. Provided that we expose students to a lot of language which they can understand the general meaning of (even though the language level is higher than their own), acquisition will successfully take place.

What would this mean for teachers if it was the most appropriate kind of language activity? It would mean that their job was simply to provide their students with the right kind of language exposure: they would not need to teach the students and the students would not have to learn.

Most teachers are convinced by the need for students to acquire language, but they also realise that students who come to language classes are in a different situation from children acquiring their first language, or from adults acquiring the language while actually living in a community which speaks the language.

Most classroom students are in a hurry: they do not have time to acquire language gradually. So while we may organise activities and material to help them acquire the language, we will also teach them language so that they *learn* it consciously.

Conclusion: Where does grammar fit in?

At this stage, it is enough to say that grammar teaching – of both the overt and covert kind – has a real and important place in the classroom. The various techniques and activities that we are going to look at in the following chapters are all useful. But then, so are communicative activities, listening and reading activities, and activities aimed directly at language acquisition. Also, teachers of EFL know that different students react differently to different kinds of methodology and technique. We are all aware, too, that different activities are useful for different purposes. So what balance should the different elements have? Which parts of the methodological programme should have the greatest weight?

In general terms we can say that, at the beginner level, we would expect to do quite a lot of structure (and function) teaching and practice and less really free communicative activity – although we would place heavy emphasis on reading and listening. The teaching of grammar at this stage is likely to be fairly covert since the main aim is to get students to practise and use the language as much as possible. As the students learn more, however, the balance would change, and at intermediate levels the students would be involved in more communicative activities and would have less grammar teaching. The teaching of grammar at this stage, however, would probably be more overt and as students get more advanced they can actively study grammar in more overt ways (for example, see many of the activities in chapter four).

At any level, though, we would expect students to be faced at various points with input that is above their own language ability. This would not only help students to acquire language subconsciously, but it could also preview language that will later form the basis for grammar teaching (see chapter four).

Exercises

1 What language functions can you think of? Select one and list as many ways of performing it as you can.
2 Look at a textbook you know and try to find a communicative activity. How do you think it would help students to learn or acquire English? How long do you think it would take?
3 Give an example of covert grammar teaching at the elementary level and an example of overt grammar teaching at the intermediate level. You can either choose examples from this book or find ones of your own.
4 Look at the task at the beginning of this unit again. Which statement do you agree with most now?

Identifying grammar: problems and solutions

People who learn languages encounter a number of problems, especially with the grammar of the language which can be complicated and which can appear confusing.

In this chapter we are going to look at three of the most important reasons for this: the clash between *function* and *form*; the similarities and differences between the students' own language and the language that is being learnt; and various exceptions and complications that all languages seem to suffer from. In each case we will discuss the problem and then consider its implications for language teaching.

Function and form

> **Task:** How many different meanings of the verb *can* are you able to think of? How would you teach *can*?

Some of the confusion about English arises because of the mismatch between *form* and *function*. For example, most teachers of English know that the present continuous tense (e.g. *he is running, they are eating their lunch*) is used to describe actions taking place now, in the present. What, then, is it being used for in these examples?

> He's meeting her at two o'clock tomorrow afternoon.
>
> Imagine the scene, exactly one year ago. It is two o'clock on a Wednesday afternoon. I am standing near the old factory . . .
>
> He's always complaining!

All these sentences use the present continuous tense, but they do not refer to the present. The first one is referring to a future arrangement, the second one is actually a story about the past, and the third one is referring to a repeated habit. The same form (present continuous) can be used to mean many different things: the form has many functions.

The situation is further complicated by the fact that the same meaning (or at least similar meanings) can be expressed by using many different forms. If we think of a situation in the future, for example, we find that it can be expressed in many different ways:

> I'll see her tomorrow.
> I'll be seeing her tomorrow.
> I'm seeing her tomorrow.
> I'm going to see her tomorrow.
> I'm to see her tomorrow.
> I see her tomorrow.

All of these grammatical constructions are different, and they all represent fine differences in meaning. The second sentence suggests that the meeting tomorrow has been definitely arranged, whereas the third sentence perhaps suggests that it is a plan, though not yet a definite arrangement. The last sentence implies that the arrangement is official.

We could go on looking at many other examples like this. As we shall see later in this chapter, it is important to be aware of such problems. Teachers have to make decisions about what structure (*form*) to teach, and what use (*function*) the structure is to be put to.

Implications for teaching

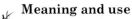

Meaning and use

It is clear that when we introduce a new piece of grammar we must teach not only the form, but also one of its functions, and not only *meaning* but also *use*. Let us return to the example of the present continuous that we looked at on page 9. We could present it by performing actions such as opening the door or closing the window. As we did these things, we could say to our students 'I am opening the door. I am closing the window'. This would certainly be an adequate demonstration of the *meaning* of the present continuous, but it wouldn't tell students how we *use* it, because people don't usually go around describing their own actions to others. But there are some situations where such commentary could be acceptable: people giving cookery demonstrations might well say what they are doing; so might the police; test pilots reporting to base; and radio commentators. Perhaps, then, it would be a better demonstration of meaning and use if we showed someone doing a cookery demonstration where they used the present continuous in an appropriate way.

Grammatical form

Teachers also have to be clear about the *grammatical form* of a new structural item. How is it formed? What are the rules? How are *If-*clauses formed, for example, or which verbs take *to* followed by the infinitive (e.g. *he agreed to wait*), which take *-ing* (e.g. *she enjoys sailing*) and which can take both (e.g. *he likes sailing/he likes to sail*)?

Patterns

Once we are clear about the function and form of the new language we then have to decide what *pattern* it is going to be taught in. In other words if we are going to introduce a grammatical item – one of the uses of a verb tense, or one of the conditional constructions, for example – we need to decide what structural patterns we are going to use to present this grammar point.

For example, we could introduce the present perfect in a number of different structural patterns:

> He's never eaten raw fish.
> I've lived here for six years.
> Since 1968 she has lived all on her own in the big house on the cliff.

We could – if we wanted – bring all these constructions into the first lesson that the students ever have on the present perfect. But if we did, the students would have to worry not only about the form of the new verb tense (*have + past participle*), but also about the use and position of time adverbials, the difference between *since* and *for*, and the position of time clauses and other long adverbial clauses. In other words, by not restricting the pattern in which the present perfect is being presented, we are making the students' task more difficult than it needs to be.

Most teachers would not teach the present perfect with *since* and *for* to begin with: indeed the difference between these two time expressions is usually introduced well after students have been presented with the new tense. Often, too, teachers do not introduce new language in a long and complicated pattern since this takes the focus away from the new language. A more sensible approach is to:

a) select the new pattern, and

b) look for examples of use which fit this pattern.

Thus in our present perfect example we might choose the pattern:

X has never + past participle, She's always + past participle

to produce sentences like, 'She's never acted in films before, she's always acted in the theatre.' Subsequent models would follow this pattern.

If we think that this pattern is too complex, we can start by introducing the tense in a much more simplified and personalised way, for example, *Have you ever . . .?* so that students ask each other, 'Have you ever met a famous person? Have you ever climbed a mountain?', etc.

In both cases the new grammar is being taught in a specific pattern, and the teacher gets students to use many sentences and/or questions using this pattern.

Contrasts with other languages

Task: Think of a language other than English. Think of at least one problem that students who speak this language have when learning English.

The second reason why English grammar is difficult for students lies in the differences between English and their own language. Take, for example, the case of Spanish and English adjectives.

Adjectives behave differently in English and Spanish, both in terms of their position and in how they agree, or don't agree, with nouns. Here are some examples:

Tengo zapatos azules.	I have blue shoes.
Mi abuela es muy vieja.	My grandmother is very old.
Me dio dos gatos pequeños.	He gave me two small cats.

English adjectives usually come before nouns (blue shoes, small cats), not after them. In Spanish the situation is reversed (*zapatos azules, gatos pequeños*). Another difference is that English adjectives do not generally change when they apply to 'masculine' or 'feminine' words or plurals. In Spanish, however, the adjective *azul* becomes *azules* when it agrees with the plural *zapatos*, *vieja* is used because it agrees with the 'feminine' grandmother (masculine *viejo*). and the singular *pequeño* becomes *pequeños*. It is not surprising that Spanish speakers have trouble with English adjectives. The situation is just as bad for English speakers who learn Spanish – and it takes most students of both languages quite a long time to get it right!

Most teachers can think of other examples: word order problems for German speakers; the use of *the, a, an* for Japanese speakers; different uses of the present perfect tense for French and Spanish speakers, and so on. Teachers with a class of students who all have the same mother tongue are in a very good position to do something about these contrasts. They can specially plan to introduce problem patterns in a particularly careful way and if necessary add a word of explanation at an appropriate stage. Teachers with multi-lingual classes will find their preparation much easier if they have some idea of any problems of contrast that their students are likely to encounter with new grammar.

Exceptions and complications

Task: Teachers frequently tell students that *some* is used with affirmative sentences and *any* is used in questions and negative sentences. Is this always true?

We now come to the third reason why English seems difficult for speakers of other languages: it is full of exceptions to grammar rules. That's the way it appears to many people, anyway. For example, when students think that they have worked out that the English past tense is formed by adding *-ed* to a verb, they are somewhat surprised to come across *went, ran* and *put*. In the same way, it seems peculiar that a noun like *sheep* does not change in the plural. It appears that all these words are 'exceptions to the rule'. The situation is not, of course, quite that simple. There are a number of English nouns that do not change when they are plural just as there are some that add an 's' (rooms, girls) while others change a sound inside the word (women, teeth).

In the same way, some nouns cannot be made plural at all, e.g. furniture, air, sugar. We don't say, for example, 'I like those two furnitures.' But then the situation does get complicated, because if we use the word 'sugar' to mean 'sugar cube' we can say, 'I'd like two sugars.' The complexity of English grammar is very depressing for some teachers – and just as worrying for their students! What can be done about it?

Teachers need to make themselves aware of the grammar they are teaching and they can do this by consulting a reference grammar (see *Suggestions for further reading* on page 69) in order to be on top of their material. In a larger sense they should make sure that the materials and books they use do not actively encourage student confusion: from the point of view of grammar, clarity is a characteristic that teachers should expect from their textbooks.

Implications for teaching

One of the most important stages of lesson preparation is where the teacher makes an attempt to predict problems which might arise and plans how to overcome them. This can be done partly from a knowledge of the students' mother tongue and the problems this will cause, and partly from previous experiences as a teacher (and the experiences of colleagues). This prediction of problems means that the teacher will have some idea of what to do when typical mistakes occur, and will have some suitable techniques to use. These two examples help to show what can be done:

1) × *He must to come tomorrow.*
   This is a common mistake that students make, often due not to interference from the mother tongue, but from confusion with the English grammatical system. We say *have to come/ought to come/want to come/would like to come*, so why not *must to* as well? A teacher who anticipates this problem can explain – if the problem arises – that verbs like *can*, *must*, *will*, and *should* are not followed by *to* whereas *have*, *ought*, *want*, *would like*, are. Hopefully this will make things clearer for the student.

2) × *I am living here since two years.*
There are two problems here: the use of the present continuous verb form and the misuse of *since*. Well-prepared teachers will not be surprised by such mistakes. They will know that the verb problem almost certainly comes from a confusion between English and the students' mother tongue. For example, whereas in French we say *J'habite ici depuis deux ans* in English we have to say 'I have lived/been living here for two years.'

Teachers also know that *since* and *for* are frequently mixed up. They are therefore prepared to explain the difference between *since + a definite point in time* and *for + a length of time*. Depending on the students, this can be done either with more examples or with grammatical explanations.

A teacher who can anticipate the problems that students are going to have, then, is in a better position to deal with these problems when they occur.

Conclusion

We have looked at three areas in which English grammar is problematical for our students. These areas should not depress us as teachers, however. Instead, we should use our knowledge of potential pitfalls to help us plan our teaching of grammar and to anticipate our students' problems. So we could use a form like this when we plan the teaching of a new grammar item:

Grammar item	
Pattern	
Concept	
Problems	
Solutions	

If we are going to teach the present perfect tense to a class of French speakers, the form might look something like this:

16

GRAMMAR ITEM	*present perfect (simple)*
PATTERN	*he/she has lived here for six years/since 198–*
CONCEPT	*a present/current state starting in the past*
PROBLEMS	*contrast with 'j'habite'/confusion with 'since' and 'for'*
SOLUTION	*(1) Use time lines to 'explain' tense* *(2) Contrast English and French to show difference* *(3) Write 'since' and 'for' on the board and note the time expressions that can go with them*

If we prepare the grammar points we are going to teach in this way, we will be in a better position to avoid the problems they may provoke. We will feel more confident as teachers and as a result we will be in a better position to help our students.

Exercises

1 What problems of form and function could there be with the modal *may*? How would your knowledge of these problems influence your decision about how to introduce *may* for the first time?
2 List three areas of grammatical difficulty between your language (or a language that you know) and English.
3 What structural pattern would you choose to teach the *going to* future for the first time?
4 How would you be able to deal with a student who always constructed questions in English like this: × *There is any cheese in the fridge?*

Presenting grammatical items

What is presentation?

Presentation is the stage at which students are introduced to the form, meaning and use of a new piece of language. They learn, for example, how *did* works with the past tense if they are being presented with past tense questions for the first time. Or they learn about the different endings of regular past tense verbs such as watched /t/, earned /d/ and landed /ɪd/. At the same time as learning how the new language is constructed, they learn what it means and how it is used. As we saw on page 10 we can easily present the meaning of a new structure; we should also try to make sure that we show how the language is used.

Presentation is the stage at which students can learn how to put the new syntax, words and sounds together. At the presentation stage, students learn the grammar that they will need for their most important experience of the new language – applying it to themselves. We call this experience *personalisation*: this is the stage at which students use a new piece of grammar to say things which really mean something to them. For example, if students have been presented with the present simple, the personalisation stage is where they apply it to themselves by saying what they do, where they live, where they go for entertainment and so on. It is often the first time students get a chance to use the new language for themselves.

Sometimes presentation takes place using personalisation immediately: the teacher uses the students and their lives to introduce new language (see example 1 page 18). Sometimes personalisation is the final part of a presentation which is done through the use of texts or pictures (see examples 2–6).

What are the characteristics of good presentation?

A good presentation should be *clear*. Students should have no difficulty in understanding the situation or what the new language means.

A good presentation should be *efficient*. The aim is to get to the personalisation stage as soon as students can manipulate the new language. The more efficiently we can do this the better.

A good presentation should be *lively* and *interesting*. We want students to get interested and be involved during a presentation stage. With the help of a good situation and lively teaching it can be one of the most memorable parts of a language course. And if it is, there is a good chance that students will remember the new grammar more easily.

A good presentation should be *appropriate*. However interesting, funny, or demonstrative a situation is, it should be appropriate for the language that is being presented. In other words it should be a good vehicle for the presentation of meaning and use.

Lastly, a good presentation should be *productive*. In other words the situation the teacher introduces should allow students to make many sentences and/or questions with the new language.

We can now look at a number of presentations that share some, or all, of the above characteristics.

1 Using charts

In this example the teacher wants to present the pattern *How does X get to work/school?* The teacher puts the following chart on the board:

Name	bus	car	train	bicycle	foot

The teacher can then ask a student 'How do you get to class?' The student chooses one of the options and the teacher writes the name in the 'name' column and ticks the appropriate 'transport' column. For example, if Juan gets to class by car, the first entry on the chart will look like this:

Name	bus	car	train	bicycle	foot
Juan		✓			

The teacher then fills up the chart with information about other students. When the chart is full he can model the question and answer:

How does Juan get to class?
By car.

> **Task:** How could you use the students and their situations to present either *whose* + *possessives* or the *going to* future.

2 Using a dialogue

> **Task:** Before looking at this example, decide how you could present *Do you like X? Yes I do/No I don't.*

In the example on page 20 for beginners from *Meridian 1*, students listen to/read a dialogue which shows the new language *Do you like . . ? Yes I do/No I don't* being used. After completing a comprehension task, students move straight onto a personalisation stage using a similar technique to the one we looked at in the first example.

This technique – of getting students to personalise the new language as soon as it is introduced – is particularly suitable for language such as: *can/can't* (= ability) where students can complete charts about each other's abilities; *possessives* + *whose* where they can ask about the 'ownership' of various objects; and *it tastes/looks/smells* + *adjective* where they can talk about their reactions to various foods, smells, etc.

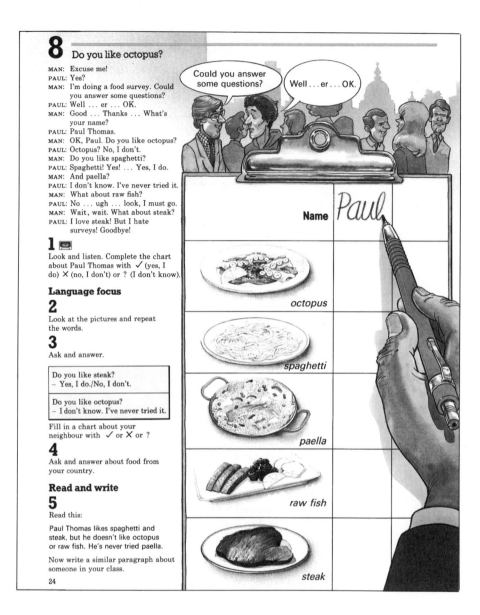

8 Do you like octopus?

MAN: Excuse me!
PAUL: Yes?
MAN: I'm doing a food survey. Could you answer some questions?
PAUL: Well ... er ... OK.
MAN: Good ... Thanks ... What's your name?
PAUL: Paul Thomas.
MAN: OK, Paul. Do you like octopus?
PAUL: Octopus? No, I don't.
MAN: Do you like spaghetti?
PAUL: Spaghetti! Yes! ... Yes, I do.
MAN: And paella?
PAUL: I don't know. I've never tried it.
MAN: What about raw fish?
PAUL: No ... ugh ... look, I must go.
MAN: Wait, wait. What about steak?
PAUL: I love steak! But I hate surveys! Goodbye!

1
Look and listen. Complete the chart about Paul Thomas with ✓ (yes, I do) ✗ (no, I don't) or ? (I don't know).

Language focus
2
Look at the pictures and repeat the words.

3
Ask and answer.

Do you like steak?
– Yes, I do./No, I don't.

Do you like octopus?
– I don't know. I've never tried it.

Fill in a chart about your neighbour with ✓ or ✗ or ?
4
Ask and answer about food from your country.

Read and write
5
Read this:

Paul Thomas likes spaghetti and steak, but he doesn't like octopus or raw fish. He's never tried paella.

Now write a similar paragraph about someone in your class.

24

3 Using a 'mini-situation'

In this example for intermediate students, the teacher wants to present the *have something done* pattern. The teacher can put these mini-situations (pictures) on the board one by one (or have them already prepared on flash cards).

Clark's Photographers	Ace Garage	Sidney: Hairdresser	Rosie Lee
'Photographs taken'	'Cars repaired'	'Hair Cut and Styled'	'Fortunes told'

Students then ask and answer like this:

Why is Mary going to Clark's photographers?
Because she wants to have her photograph taken.

For a personalisation stage, the students can say what they would like to *have done*, e.g. 'I'd like to have my hair cut'.

> **Task:** What other question and answer models will the students have to produce for the pictures above using *have something done*.
> What other mini-situations/pictures can you think of to introduce this pattern?

4 Using texts for contrast

> **Task:** Before looking at the example, decide what the difference is between the use of the future simple and the future continuous tenses. How could you make this clear to the students?

In this example for intermediate students from *English in Situations*, students read a text which provides situations that allow them to contrast the future continuous and the future simple tenses.

i. Lord Kane, an important British diplomat, must fly to Washington immediately on an emergency mission. A government car is taking him to London airport now. A special plane is already waiting. Everything is ready for an immediate take-off,
THE PLANE WILL BE WAITING FOR HIM WHEN HE GET THERE
IT WILL TAKE OFF WHEN HE GETS THERE

1. Who is Lord Kane?
2. What is happening now?
3. Why is there all this rush?
4. What is the crew of the plane doing now?
5. Ask what they'll be doing when he gets there!
6. Ask what they'll do!

---

ii. 3 police cars are speeding through the night. They have just received information that a notorious criminal is playing roulette at this very moment in a gambling club.
HE'LL BE PLAYING ROULETTE WHEN THEY GET THERE
HE'LL RUN AWAY WHEN THEY GET THERE

1. Why are the police cars in such a hurry?
2. What is the criminal doing at this moment?
3. Ask 2 questions about him with WILL BE DOING and WILL DO WHEN THEY GET THERE!

iii. It is only a few seconds before 4 o'clock in the factory where Bill works. All the men are working hard but they know that the whistle always blows at exactly 4 o'clock. They always stop then and rush home.
THEY WILL ALL BE WORKING WHEN THE WHISTLE BLOWS. THEY WILL ALL STOP WHEN IT BLOWS.

1. What time is it?
2. What always happens at 4?
3. What are the men doing now?
4. What will they be doing when the whistle blows?
5. What will they do?

As a personalisation stage, students can say what they will be doing/what they will do at a certain time in the future (e.g. eight o'clock tomorrow evening, lunchtime next Sunday).

5 Using texts for grammar explanation

Task: Before looking at this example, decide how much grammatical explanation you would give when presenting the present perfect with *since* and *for*. How could you give this information?

In this example from *Kernel 2*, elementary students read a text which gives examples of the new language (present perfect with *since* and *for*). The grammar is then explained before they are asked to choose between *since* and *for*. This is the text:

Our other story this evening is the weather. For the last five days it has been below zero in most parts of the country. Cold, frost and heavy snow have caused terrible problems everywhere. Everyone is asking the same question – 'When will it end?'

Well, the weatherman predicts it won't last much longer. Better weather is on the way. The temperature will rise above zero tomorrow. And we'll see the sun again for a few hours. There'll be more about this, too, in our special weather report at the end of the programme.

And this is the explanation and preliminary exercise:

1 Stop and look.

1 It has been cold **for** five days.

MONDAY TUESDAY WEDNESDAY THURSDAY FRIDAY

It has been cold **since** last Monday.

Use *for* when you are talking about a length of time.
(————) *Five days, ten years, three hours* are all lengths of time.
Use *since* when you point back to the point in time (←———)
when something began.

2 Use since or for.

1 It is eleven o'clock. The man has been waiting for the bus
_____ 10.30.
2 In other words, he has been there _____ half an hour.
3 The woman has been waiting _____ only ten minutes.
4 In other words, she has been waiting _____ 10.50.
5 The man has been waiting _____ a longer time than the
woman.

For personalisation, the students can ask each other how long they have done various things. They will answer with *since* or *for*.

6 Using visuals for situations

A final example shows how teachers can use pictures for structural presentation. This material is for elementary students who are going to learn the past continuous tense for the first time. The teacher can gradually draw this picture on the board:

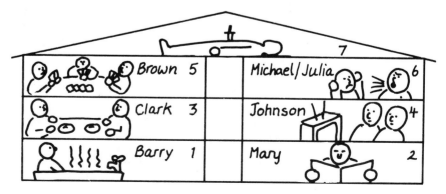

The students discover that a murder took place at exactly eight o'clock in the top flat of a block of flats. They will ask and answer, like this:

> What were the Johnsons doing in flat 4 at eight o'clock?
> They were watching television.

Task: How could you complete this presentation sequence with a personalisation phase?

What overt grammatical help can the teacher give at the presentation stage?

In two of our examples (1 and 5) we have seen that the materials give the students a considerable amount of grammatical information. But where materials do not give this kind of information, or where teachers are using pictures or their own realia, they will often want to give extra grammar information themselves. How can this be done?

Modelling

One technique is for the teacher to give a clear spoken model of the new language. This should be done with normal speed, stress and intonation. The teacher can give this model a number of times and then ask students to repeat it, both in chorus and individually. The modelling is particularly important since it gives students a chance to hear what the new sentence should really sound like. Repeating in chorus allows students to 'have a go' at the new language without having to talk individually in front of the class.

Isolation

Teachers frequently isolate parts of the sentence they are modelling so that they can give them special emphasis. When teachers present the first conditional, for example, they might model a sentence like this:

> If it rains, she'll get wet . . . listen, she'll . . . she will . . . she'll . . . she'll get wet. If it rains, she'll get wet.

The teacher isolated the *she'll* element, and then explained what it was (she will) before putting it back into the model that was being given. Students get a lot of grammatical information in this way, although rules are not specifically stated.

Visual demonstration

Another way of explaining grammar is through various forms of visual demonstration. In example 5 we saw how a diagram could be coupled with an explanation to give a clear demonstration of the point being made.

Other diagrammatic/visual demonstrations that can be used are:

Writing

The teacher can write sentences on the board and underline the critical points. Relationships between questions and answers, for example, can be shown with arrows and boxes like this:

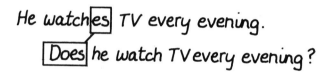

Time lines

A favourite technique for many teachers is the use of time lines, where a diagrammatic representation of tense and aspect is given. Thus the present perfect continuous in the sentence *I've been reading the newspaper* might look like this (it is represented by the dotted line):

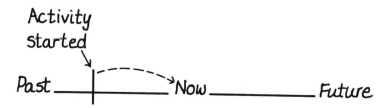

Whereas the time line for the future perfect tense in the sentence *In two months I will have seen most of the United States* could look like this:

2 months from 'Now'

Past _____ Now _____ ___ Future

Fingers

Many teachers use hands and fingers as a way of demonstrating grammatical structure. For example, if we consider how *will* is frequently contracted, we might be focussing on a sentence like *She'll arrive tomorrow*. After modelling it, the teacher holds up four fingers and says this sentence, pointing to a finger for each word:

She will arrive tomorrow

The teacher then puts fingers 1 and 2 together and now says (pointing with the other hand):

She'll arrive tomorrow

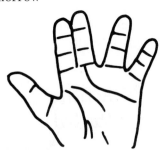

The act of pointing can also be used to increase the students' speed, rhythm and stress.

The same effect is often achieved by teachers using Cuisenaire rods. Originally developed for use with a method called the Silent Way, these rods are of different colours and lengths. Teachers can give different grammatical properties to different rods and thus help to make grammar learning more visual.

Explanation

Of course teachers frequently explain new grammar. This can be done more or less overtly (see page 3). The use of 'isolation' (see above) is obviously a fairly covert way of explaining, whereas the following explanation is more overt:

> We don't usually put adverbs between the verb and its object. Actually there are three main positions for adverbs: mid-position; end position; or initial position. We put adverbs in initial position when . . .

This explanation might well present problems to a lot of students because of the technical words being used, and because abstract grammar explanations are always quite difficult to swallow. Of course, said in the students' mother tongue it would be a lot more comprehensible. But we will want to be careful about the amount of mother tongue that we use in the English class.

In general it seems that grammar explanations for beginners and elementary students are better handled with more obvious techniques, such as isolation and demonstration. Of course this is not always the case, and where a rule is easy to explain at the students' level, then clearly an explanation would be appropriate.

Conclusion

In this chapter we have said that *presentation* is the stage at which students are introduced to the form, meaning and use of the new language. We have said that good presentations should be clear, efficient, lively and interesting, appropriate and productive. We have looked at examples of presentation material and concluded by looking at ways in which the teacher can give students more grammatical information.

Exercises

1 Look at the exercise on page 18 again. What problem might be caused by the words at the top of the chart and what mistake can you predict? How could you solve this problem?
2 You have to present the past simple tense.
   a) How can you do this using the students and their situations?
   b) Look at some textbooks and see how they introduce the structure for the first time. Choose the one you like best and decide how you would teach it.
3 How would you use time lines to help students understand the difference between the past simple and the past continuous tenses?
4 How would you use your hands and fingers to demonstrate the contracted form of *would* and *have* in a third conditional sentence like: *If I'd known I'd've come earlier.*

References

The examples from textbooks in this chapter come from the following books:

Meridian. Student's Book 1 by Jeremy Harmer, p 24 (Longman 1985)
English in Situations by Robert O'Neill, p 138 (Oxford University Press 1970)
Kernel 2 by Robert O'Neill, pp 37, 38 (Longman 1982)

Discovery techniques

In this chapter we are going to look at exercises and techniques which encourage students to 'discover' facts about grammar and grammatical usage.

What are discovery techniques?

In the last chapter we looked at ways in which the teacher asks the student to focus on new items of language. It was the teacher's job to give the students examples of the language which the students then repeated and used. The teacher explained the grammatical and phonological form of the new language through various techniques.

Discovery techniques, on the other hand, are those where students are given examples of language and told to find out how they work – to *discover* the grammar rules rather than be told them. At the most covert level, this simply means that the students are exposed to the new language, with no focus or fuss, some time before it is presented. At a more conscious level, students can be asked to look at some sentences and say how the meaning is expressed and what the differences are between the sentences. As students puzzle through the information and solve the problem in front of them, they find out how grammar is used in a text and are actually acquiring a grammar rule. The advantages of this approach are clear. By involving the students' reasoning processes in the task of grammar acquisition, we make sure that they are concentrating fully, using their cognitive powers. We are also ensuring that our approach is more student-centred: it's not just the teacher telling the students what the grammar is. They are actually discovering information for themselves.

Of course these techniques are not suitable for all students on all occasions. Discovery activities can take a long time and can occasionally be confusing. The teacher should decide when to use these activities, with what grammar, and with which students.

Most teachers and materials writers have found, of course, that this kind of material is easy to design and use at intermediate levels where students have more English to 'talk about' language. For this reason, many of the examples below come from materials for lower intermediate students and above, rather than from books for beginners. But as we shall see, there are also ways of using discovery techniques at lower levels.

We will be looking at four types of activity: preview; matching techniques; text study; and problem-solving.

Preview

One rather disguised and covert way of allowing students to discover new grammar for themselves is to preview it at some stage before it is actively learnt and taught. In other words, students are exposed to the new language; they do not concentrate on it at this stage, but the fact of having seen the grammar 'in action' will help them to deal with it when they have to study it later.

Activities such as reading and listening to texts expose students to language in this way, because while students are practising listening and reading skills, they can also be absorbing new language. These two examples from textbooks show this kind of preview in action:

1) from *Track 2*

> **Task:** Search the text and see how many examples of *If-* clauses you can find.

In this extract (from the second stage of a course for adolescents) the text contains examples of the grammatical patterns to be taught in subsequent classes, patterns such as: *If it rains on Sunday I'll stay at home/What will you do if it's sunny?* In other words, the text is used not only for comprehension and for setting up a topic for use later in the unit, but also to make the students familiar with the new language before teaching it later.

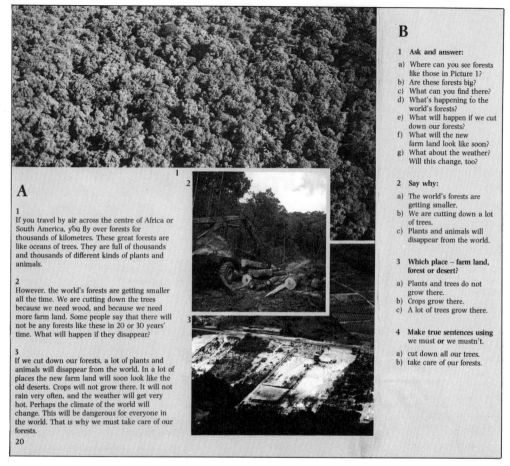

B

1 Ask and answer:

a) Where can you see forests like those in Picture 1?
b) Are these forests big?
c) What can you find there?
d) What's happening to the world's forests?
e) What will happen if we cut down our forests?
f) What will the new farm land look like soon?
g) What about the weather? Will this change, too?

2 Say why:

a) The world's forests are getting smaller.
b) We are cutting down a lot of trees.
c) Plants and animals will disappear from the world.

3 Which place – farm land, forest or desert?

a) Plants and trees do not grow there.
b) Crops grow there.
c) A lot of trees grow there.

4 Make true sentences using we must or we mustn't.

a) cut down all our trees.
b) take care of our forests.

A

1
If you travel by air across the centre of Africa or South America, you fly over forests for thousands of kilometres. These great forests are like oceans of trees. They are full of thousands and thousands of different kinds of plants and animals.

2
However, the world's forests are getting smaller all the time. We are cutting down the trees because we need wood, and because we need more farm land. Some people say that there will not be any forests like these in 20 or 30 years' time. What will happen if they disappear?

3
If we cut down our forests, a lot of plants and animals will disappear from the world. In a lot of places the new farm land will soon look like the old deserts. Crops will not grow there. It will not rain very often, and the weather will get very hot. Perhaps the climate of the world will change. This will be dangerous for everyone in the world. That is why we must take care of our forests.

20

2) from *Meridian. Student's Book 1*

> **Task:** Read through the text (which comes from halfway through a beginners' course). What language is being previewed here, do you think?

In the example on page 32, the students are practising the skill of extracting facts and figures from a piece of text. At the same time, though, there are two uses of *can*, expressing possibility, which will be the focus of study in a subsequent lesson.

Previewing, then, is a way of making students aware of a new piece of language: this will help them when they study it at a later stage.

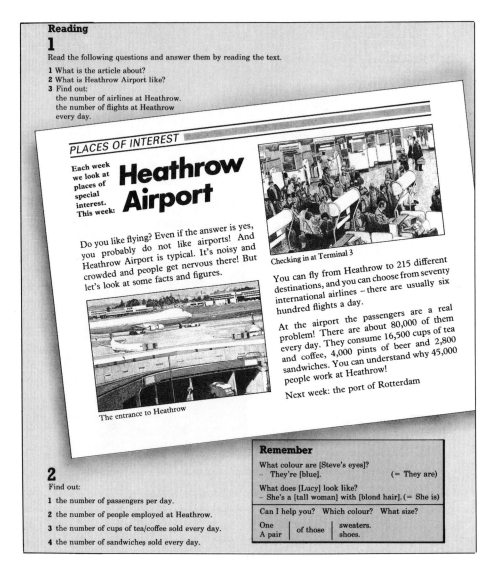

Reading

1

Read the following questions and answer them by reading the text.

1 What is the article about?
2 What is Heathrow Airport like?
3 Find out:
   the number of airlines at Heathrow.
   the number of flights at Heathrow
   every day.

PLACES OF INTEREST

Each week
we look at
places of
special
interest.
This week:

Heathrow Airport

Do you like flying? Even if the answer is yes, you probably do not like airports! And Heathrow Airport is typical. It's noisy and crowded and people get nervous there! But let's look at some facts and figures.

Checking in at Terminal 3

You can fly from Heathrow to 215 different destinations, and you can choose from seventy international airlines – there are usually six hundred flights a day.

At the airport the passengers are a real problem! There are about 80,000 of them every day. They consume 16,500 cups of tea and coffee, 4,000 pints of beer and 2,800 sandwiches. You can understand why 45,000 people work at Heathrow!

Next week: the port of Rotterdam

The entrance to Heathrow

2

Find out:

1 the number of passengers per day.
2 the number of people employed at Heathrow.
3 the number of cups of tea/coffee sold every day.
4 the number of sandwiches sold every day.

Remember

What colour are [Steve's eyes]?
- They're [blue].   (= They are)

What does [Lucy] look like?
- She's a [tall woman] with [blond hair]. (= She is)

Can I help you?	Which colour?	What size?
One A pair	of those	sweaters. shoes.

Matching techniques

A number of grammar exercises ask students to match parts of sentences and phrases. Often they work in pairs for this and treat the activity rather like a problem-solving exercise (see page 37).

The point of matching exercises is to get students to work things out for themselves: they have to make choices about what goes with what, and the activity of making choices helps them to discover correct facts about grammar. These two examples show matching exercises:

1) Tag questions
In this matching exercise for elementary learners, the students have to match sentences with the tag questions that would go with them. As they do this (individually or in pairs) they work out how tag questions work.

You've been to Brazil,   are you?
You can play the flute,   don't you?
You study economics,   did you?
You aren't going to leave,   haven't you?
You didn't fail the exam,   can't you?

Task: Select another grammatical area that you could use the same technique for.

2) from *Ways to Grammar*
In this example from a grammar book for intermediate students, the use of the word *unless* is briefly explained. Students are then asked to do a matching exercise. While they are doing this, they will be sorting out their understanding of *unless* and how it compares with *if*.

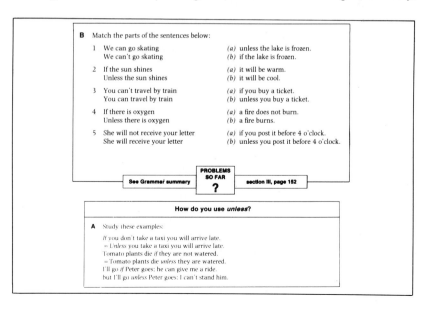

> **Task:** Select another grammatical area that you could use the same technique for.

Text study

Another way of getting students to discover new grammar is to ask them to concentrate on its use in a text. Teachers can get students to look at the way language is used – or what kind of language is used in a certain context. The principle aim here is to get students to recognise the new language. Three contrasting examples will show this technique:

1) from *Kernel 1*

> **Task:** Decide what the new grammar point is in the second passage.

In this extract, students have a situation clearly set up by the two short passages of text. The new grammar point is then brought into the second short passage for immediate student attention.

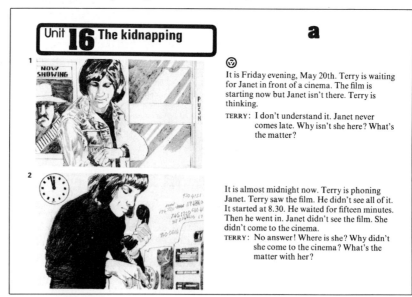

Unit **16** The kidnapping

a

It is Friday evening, May 20th. Terry is waiting for Janet in front of a cinema. The film is starting now but Janet isn't there. Terry is thinking.

TERRY: I don't understand it. Janet never comes late. Why isn't she here? What's the matter?

It is almost midnight now. Terry is phoning Janet. Terry saw the film. He didn't see all of it. It started at 8.30. He waited for fifteen minutes. Then he went in. Janet didn't see the film. She didn't come to the cinema.

TERRY: No answer! Where is she? Why didn't she come to the cinema? What's the matter with her?

This type of material is very similar, of course, to the presentation material we looked at in chapter three. Here, as part of the presentation, the material asks students to discover for themselves what the grammar is, and what it means.

2) from *Turtle Diary*

Perhaps the best kind of text study is where students read (or listen to) an authentic piece of text and then search through it to see how certain concepts are referred to.

> **Task:** What concepts or verb tenses in this text would you point out to a group of lower intermediate students?

> I saw a film once, *The Swimmer*, with Burt Lancaster. In it he was an American advertising man whose mind had slipped out of the present. He thought he still had a wife and children and a house, but it was all gone. The film began with a golden late-summer afternoon. He turned up at the swimming pool of some friends who hadn't seen him for a long time. They looked at him strangely, he wasn't part of their present time any more. While he was there it occurred to him that there were so many swimming pools in that part of Connecticut that he could almost swim all the way home. So he went from pool to pool, public and private, swimming across Fairfield County meeting people from different bits of his life whilst swimming home as he thought. And wherever he went people became angry and disturbed, he didn't belong in their present time, they didn't want him in it. At the end of the film he was huddled in the doorway of the empty locked house that had been his while rain came down and he heard the ball going back and forth on the empty tennis court and the voices of his daughters who were gone. Dora and I saw the film together.
>
> © Russell Hoban 1975

Students read this extract from the novel *Turtle Diary* by Russell Hoban. After they have done comprehension exercises and discussed the extract, the teacher can ask them to look at the following sentences:

> In it he was an American advertising man whose mind had slipped out of the present.

> He turned up at the swimming pool of some friends who hadn't seen him for a long time.

> At the end of the film he was huddled in the doorway of the empty locked house that had been his.

They can then be asked to identify the verb (in each sentence) that refers to time/events *before* the film and the verb (in each sentence) which refers to time/events *during* the film. Clearly the past perfect forms are the 'before the film' verbs and the past simple verbs are the 'during the film' verbs.

The point about this kind of activity is that the teacher asks the students to work something out for themselves. They see language in its proper (authentic) context and are then led to understand how it works.

The same technique can be used with newspaper articles, play extracts, poetry, advertisements, etc.

3) The past simple

> **Task:** What are the three past endings for regular verbs?

In this example, students read a text and then have to select the verb endings and put the verbs in the right columns according to their endings.

First of all the teacher writes a text using the required verbs. Here is an example:

> Mary watched the old man. He walked down the road. He stopped and talked to Mrs Castle at number 27. Then he crossed the road and managed to dodge the traffic. He visited the drugstore and disappeared through the door. Then he reappeared and walked towards her.

The students have to put all the verbs into one of the three columns:

/d/	/t/	/ɪd/
managed	watched	visited

This activity would be suitable either before, or immediately after, a presentation of the past simple. The advantage of using it before the presentation is that it will give students a clear knowledge of the tense before they are asked to use it. If used after, it will serve as a good reinforcement to what the students have been learning. Either way, the fact that students are asked to complete this exercise themselves means that they are personally very involved in the acquisition of grammatical knowledge about the different endings of regular past tense verbs.

This kind of overt and conscious study of grammatical form leads us into our final category of discovery techniques.

Problem-solving

As students move from beginner levels of English through to intermediate and beyond, their level of English allows us to encourage them to talk about grammar and to analyse its properties. More importantly perhaps, students can look at areas of grammar rather than small details; the future, for example, rather than just one future form such as *going to*. One way of getting students to do this is to set up a problem and ask students to solve it. The problem can be, for example, that six sentences use the same structure, but it has six different meanings – what are they? Or the problem concerns typical mistakes that students make – how can they be corrected? The three examples we shall look at here show how, in solving such problems, students become aware of how the grammar of English works.

1) from *Ways to Grammar*
In this extract, we assume that students already have some

How do you refer to future time?

A   Study these examples:

1   Goodbye. *I'll see* you tomorrow.
2   Look at those big black clouds: it's *going to rain*.
3   We bought our tickets yesterday. *We're leaving* at 4 o'clock this afternoon.
4   Beth *may come* to stay with us next weekend.
5   The weather *might be* better if we wait until July.
6   Our boat *leaves* Southampton at 10 am next Monday and *arrives* in New York next Friday evening.

B   Now write the numbers of the examples above in the appropriate columns:

the speaker is sure: the speaker is not sure:

See Grammar summary   **PROBLEMS SO FAR ?**   sections I, II and III, page 115 knowledge of the various ways of expressing the future. What is important is to get them to see the differences of meaning and use. This exercise asks them to study the future in terms of how sure the speaker is of the future.

> **Task:** Decide what level you could use this exercise at and how easy the students would find it.

2) from *Discover English*

In these examples, the students are encouraged to become aware of exactly the kind of aspects of grammar that we discussed in chapter two – the problems of form and function. In the first exercise (A), students are encouraged to realise that all the sentences refer to habitual or repeated actions, even though the grammatical forms are different. In the second exercise (B), students will recognise that the same form (the present continuous) can be used to express a number of different meanings.

> ### SECTION TWO
>
> Look at these groups of utterances. What do the utterances in each group have in common? What distinguishes them? If necessary, check in the commentary after doing exercise **A** to see whether you are on the right track.
>
> **A.**
> 1. Willy smokes
> 2. Fred's a slow worker.
> 3. Aggie used to drink.
> 4. Joe's in the habit of talking in his sleep.
> 5. He's always making that mistake.
>
> **B.**
> 1. Pollution is getting worse.
> 2. It's raining.
> 3. I'm going out tonight.
> 4. He's always dropping ash on the carpet.

> **Task:** How would you use this material in class?

3) Using students' efforts

> **Task:** List three of the most common verb tense mistakes that your elementary students make.

A very good way of getting students to discover grammatical rules is to present them with examples of incorrect English. You can then encourage them to discover what is wrong and why. Here are two possible ways of doing this:

1 While students are involved in an oral activity, go round the class noting down any errors you hear. When they have finished you can choose the mistakes that are the most 'serious' and write them up on the board, like this:

1 x You must to agree with me

2 x People is always complaining

3 x I haven't seen him yesterday

4 x I am not agree

Now students can work in pairs to identify the mistakes and put them right. (Notice that you should not say who made the mistakes.)
2 When students have written a composition (such as a letter, narrative, or advertisement) choose one which contains some common mistakes. Wipe out the name on the homework, underline the mistakes, and then photocopy it. In groups, students can study the composition and decide why the underlined pieces are wrong, and how to correct them.

Conclusion

Encouraging students to discover grammar for themselves is one valuable way of helping them to get to grips with the language. Very often this discovering of grammatical facts involves students in a fairly analytical study of the language – especially in the more intermediate examples we looked at. Teachers will have to decide how much of this kind of material is appropriate for their students, but one thing is certain: the use of discovery techniques can be highly motivating and extremely beneficial for the students' understanding of English grammar. So then the question is whether these techniques are particularly time-consuming. Obviously reading a text (see pages 31, 32 and 35) takes time, but teachers should remember that the student will get reading practice as well as focusing on the grammar. Getting students to solve grammatical problems probably seems like a very long process. But if we think of the amount of time we generally spend on presentation at the intermediate level, the use of a problem-solving activity does not seem exaggerated.

So time is not really a problem. What is much more important is whether teachers feel happy with these techniques and whether or not they suit the students.

Exercises

1 Find an authentic English text that would be suitable for your students.
   a) Study it to see what language you could draw students' attention to.
   b) How would you draw the students' attention to the concept/language you have selected?
2 Choose a structure and a pattern.
   a) Write a story using examples of the structure.
   b) Decide on the task the students will do which will help them to recognise the structure (see example 3, page 36).
3 Listen to some students talking and write down every mistake you hear. Decide which of these mistakes you would put up on the board if you were going to use the techniques described on page 39.

References

The examples in this chapter have come from the following books:
Track 2 by Michael Palmer and Donn Byrne, pp 20, 21 (Longman 1982)
Meridian Student's Book 1 by Jeremy Harmer, p 35 (Longman 1985)
Ways to Grammar by John Shepherd, Richard Rossner and James Taylor, pp 143, 144, 112 (Macmillan 1984)
Kernel 1 by Robert O'Neill, p 83 (Longman 1979)
Turtle Diary by Russell Hoban, pp 70, 71 (Picador Books 1975)
Discover English by Rod Bolitho and Brian Tomlinson, p 8 (Heinemann 1980)

Practice techniques

In this chapter we are going to look at exercises and techniques which get students to practise grammatical items. In each case the teacher or the textbook writer has decided that certain specific items of language should be practised. But there are various ways of doing this. Some of them are straightforward – like drills – and others are more involved such as the use of interaction activities, games and quizzes.

We will be looking at four different types of oral practice: drills; interaction activities; involving the personality; and games. We will also be looking at some written practice activities.

Drills

The aim of a drill is to give students rapid practice in using a structural item. Often this is done with the whole class – rather than with students in pairs – and the teacher is able to get students to ask and answer questions quickly and efficiently. The chief advantage of this kind of technique is that teachers can correct any mistakes that the students make and can encourage them to concentrate on difficulties at the same time. The problem with drills is that they are often not very creative. Teachers should make sure that they are not overused and that they do not go on for too long. As soon as students show that they can make correct sentences with the new item, the teacher should move onto more creative activities like the interaction activities in the next section. These two examples show drills in action:

1) Lists – *have to* and *would like to*
Teachers can create material for controlled practice with drawings/mini-situations on the board just as they can create presentation material.

42

In this example the teacher draws two faces on the board and gives them names. Then he or she writes in prompts for what the characters *have to* do at work and what they *would like to* do. For example:

	Jake	Miss Greystoke
Obligations	Clean floors Wash windows Empty rubbish	Type letters Answer the telephone Take shorthand
Desires	Marry Miss Greystoke Learn to read Get a better job	Earn more money Take a long holiday Marry her boss

Students now practise asking and answering.

What does Jake have to do at work? He has to clean floors.
What would he like to do? He'd like to marry Miss Greystoke.

Task: How long would you let this activity continue? Would you use pairwork or do it with the whole class together?

2) From *Meanings into Words: Intermediate*

8.6 RECENT ACTIVITIES AND ACHIEVEMENTS   Practice

Work in pairs.

Example A: You look tired. What have you been doing?
B: I've been redecorating my flat.
A: How much have you done?
How far have you got with it?
B: Well, so far I've done the ceiling and I've papered the walls, but I haven't painted the woodwork yet.

Have conversations like this about:

1 cleaning the living room
2 typing letters
3 revising for the exam
4 building a house
5 making the supper
6 getting the flat ready for a party
7 organising your brother's wedding

Work in groups. Tell each other what you have really been doing recently, and what particular things you have done.

In this example at the intermediate level students are practising the present perfect continuous and they are given more freedom than in the previous example to use their own ideas.

Notice that the instruction is for the students to work in pairs. Here the teacher would first conduct the drill working with the whole class. With the first prompt 'cleaning the living room' the teacher can hold up cards with words like 'dust the furniture/vacuum the carpet/shake out the rugs' as prompts for the students to say, 'Well, so far I've dusted the furniture and hoovered the carpets, I haven't shaken out the rugs yet.' The teacher would then continue to give prompts where necessary until the students showed that they understood and could do the drill. At that moment the teacher would put them into pairs to continue the exercise.

> **Task:** What other drills can you think of?

Drills, then, are fairly mechanical ways of getting students to demonstrate and practise their ability to use specific language items in a controlled manner.

Interaction activities

One of the problems about drills is that they are fairly monotonous. Some way must be found of making controlled language practice more meaningful and more enjoyable. One of the ways of doing this is by using interaction activities. These are designed so that students work together, exchanging information in a purposeful and interesting way. The following two examples show exercises which get students to practise grammatical items in a motivating way.

1) From *Coast to Coast 1*
In this (American English) example at beginner level, students are practising *where* questions with the present simple, making a difference between third person singular and plural verb endings.

Students are put in pairs. Student A looks at the following material:

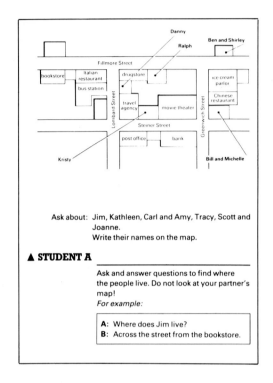

Ask about: Jim, Kathleen, Carl and Amy, Tracy, Scott and Joanne.
Write their names on the map.

▲ **STUDENT A** _____

Ask and answer questions to find where the people live. Do not look at your partner's map!
For example:

> **A:** Where does Jim live?
> **B:** Across the street from the bookstore.

Student B looks at a slightly different map:

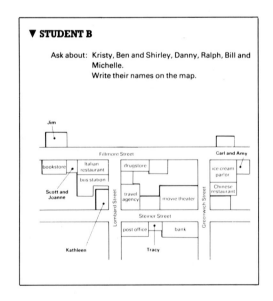

▼ **STUDENT B**

Ask about: Kristy, Ben and Shirley, Danny, Ralph, Bill and Michelle.
Write their names on the map.

You will notice that A and B's information is slightly different. For example, A doesn't know where Tracy lives and has to ask B, who does know. B doesn't know where Ben and Shirley live and has to ask A. The whole point is that A and B *must not look at each other's maps* until they have finished. So the only way they have of completing the task is by asking each other questions like (A) 'Where does Tracy live?' to which B will reply, 'Between the post office and the bank'.

This is an example of a so-called *information gap* activity – where students have to ask each other for information to 'close the gap' in the information which they both have.

> **Task:** Decide what instructions you would give your class to make sure that this activity was a success.

2) Charts – past and present tenses
Charts are very useful to promote interaction between students; in order to complete them the students have to question each other and note down the replies.

In this example students have to write down another student's name. Then they ask that student these questions:

> What is your favourite leisure activity?
> When did you last (do your favourite leisure activity)?
> How often do you (do your favourite leisure activity)?

They fill in this chart according to the answers:

	Name	Favourite leisure activity	When?	How often?
1				
2				
3				
4				
5				

The best way of doing this activity is to ask all the students to stand up. They can then move round the class questioning various classmates. When the students have finished they can compare results. What is the most popular leisure activity in the class?

> **Task:** Decide what problems this activity might cause. How could you overcome them?

Involving the personality

Recently some teachers and materials writers have designed exercises which practise grammar while at the same time requiring students to talk about themselves in a more involved way than in the example above. They are asked to discuss things that affect their personality and to use this subject matter as a focus for grammar practice. These two examples show how this can be done:

1) Chain drill – crimes[1]
One way of making a practice drill more involving is to get students to contribute something of their own to it; in this way they will be more involved in the practice (even though it is fairly mechanical).

In this example, students are practising the present perfect. They sit in circles and one after the other have to say,

> *I am* (name) *and I've never* (crime),
> for example, 'I am Maria and I've never robbed a bank.'

This activity is great fun, although if the circle is too large the students soon run out of 'crimes' and have to think fairly hard. Some people also worry that students might reveal a bit too much of themselves when they choose the crime that they haven't committed!

> **Task:** Do you like this activity? Why? Why not?

2) Your favourite food
In this example from *Caring and Sharing in the Foreign Language Class*, students practise the use of *was* and *were* in the context of talking about their childhood in a positive and happy light. In an

activity like this teachers may find that even at a very basic level students start discussing rather than practising the language.

Procedures: begin the activity by talking about childhood memories:

"We all have a number of childhood memories that made us happy in some way. As we get older, we tend not to think about them very much. Yet to do so helps us relive the good feelings we had at the time.

"Today we're going to recall some of our favorite things from childhood. Each of you will have a handout listing some categories. In your groups take one category at a time. The first person will ask the second person a question, such as 'What was your favorite candy?' The second person answers and then asks the first person the same question. It will now be time to start a new round of questions. Rotate who asks the questions first each time so the same person does not do so always.

"In some cases, your answers will be brief. For other questions, they will be longer. You can ask one another additional questions or add comments, if you wish. You will find as your partner answers that other memories will come back to you. When you finish all of the questions on the handout, add some of your own categories to the list and take some extra turns using them."

Pass out the dittos. Here are some possible categories that can be used:

WHEN YOU WERE A CHILD, WHAT (OR WHO) WAS YOUR FAVORITE:

1. Toy? Why?
2. Holiday? Why?
3. Food? Candy? Why?
4. Play activity?
5. Book or story? Why?
6. Place to go? Why?
7. Song?
8. Outfit?
9. TV programs? Radio programs? Why?
10. Hobby?
11. Friend? Why?
12. Grownup (other than family)? Why?
13. Teacher? Why?
14. Relative (not a parent or guardian)? Why?
15. Memory of snow?
16. Memory at a beach or pool?
17. Thing to do that was scary?
18. Birthday? Why?
19. Comic strip?
20. Ride at the amusement park?

Task: This material is from an American writer. How can you tell?

In both these examples the practice has been designed to be more interesting than usual. Because the students are themselves involved in what they are talking about, the activities are likely to be more meaningful. However, teachers have to be sure that their students are mature enough to handle such activities and they need to be sensitive to the students' reactions to such exercises.

Games

Games of various kinds have been used in language teaching for a long time and they are especially useful for grammar work.

48

Task: Have you ever used games in class to practise language? Did you ever play games in class when you were learning a language?

Noughts and crosses/tic-tac-toe

This game is very popular in the classroom – as it is in real life. The class is divided into teams. Team A uses the nought (0) and team B uses the cross (X). The teacher draws a grid on the board and fills each space with a word or phrase. For example, if the teacher wanted to practise question words, the board might look like this:

what	how	when
when	why	how
why	what	why

Team A chooses one of the squares and one of the team has to make a sentence or question with the word or phrase in that square. If they succeed they put an 0 on that square. Team B tries to do the same with another square; if they are successful they put a cross on their square. The first team to get a straight line of three noughts or crosses (either horizontally, vertically or diagonally) wins the game.

Teachers can of course put whatever words they want in the spaces, for example, modal verbs, infinitives which the students have to make into past verbs, conjunctions, etc.

General knowledge quizzes

General knowledge quizzes can be very enjoyable and can be used to practise various grammatical items. Here is a procedure to follow if the teacher of an elementary class wants the students to practise the superlative form of adjectives.

The teacher elicits superlative adjectives (e.g. oldest, biggest, longest, most expensive) from the students. They then divide into two teams. Each team must write general knowledge questions using these adjectives, such as 'What is the highest mountain in the world?' While they are writing these questions they can consult atlases and other reference books. When the game starts, team A asks team B one of the questions. Team B gets a point if they answer correctly.

Quizzes can also be used for past tenses, ('Who was the first man on the moon?'), comparatives, ('Which is heavier; an elephant or a whale?') and so on.

Board games

Many board games have been adapted for use in English teaching. The following game, taken from *Meridian 2*, is a typical example of such games.

The board looks like this:

These are the instructions which the student gets:

3 : :

Meridian Trail:
a game for 3–5 players

You need:
* a dice
* the Trail board on page 74–75
* a small piece of paper with your name on it to use as a 'counter'

How to play
1 Throw the dice. The player with the top score starts the game.
2 The player throws the dice. If, for example, the dice shows 4, he goes forward four squares.
3 If a player lands on, for example, a *GO TO 6* square, he goes forward to square number 6. If he lands on a *GO BACK TO 3* square, he goes back to square number 3.
4 When a player lands on a *RISK* square, all the players must look at the *RISK* questions on page 75. For unit 10 the player must choose the number between 1 and 10 on the *RISK* square and answer the question. If the other players say 'correct', he goes forward one square. If they say 'wrong', he goes back one square. If in doubt, ask the teacher.
5 The winner is the first player at number 30.

And these are the questions which the students have to answer if they land on a 'risk' square:

Meridian Trail: Risks 1–10

1 Complete the sequence:
tall/taller/tallest; big/bigger/biggest; good/........./..........
2 Which is correct? He isn't as **a** *bigger* **b** *biggest* **c** *big* as his brother.
3 Complete this sentence:
Books are .... expensive than records.
4 Complete the sequence:
wear/wore/worn; work/worked/worked; kick/........./..........; go/........./..........
5 Give the correct form of the verb in brackets:
I (never see) .... the film 'A Passage to India'.
6 Make a sentence with *just.*
7 Complete this sentence with one word only:
I haven't got .... money.
8 Complete the following sequence:
kind/unkind; expensive/inexpensive; possible/..........
9 Make a question with *most expensive.*
10 Which is correct? He **a** *has* **b** *was* just been made President.

Meridian Trail: Risks 11–20

11 Complete this sentence with one word only:
   You weren't at home last night, ... you?
12 Give the correct form of the verb in brackets:
   Next week I (buy) a new car.
13 Make a question with *been*.
14 Which is correct? I haven't seen him   **a** *since*   **b** *for*   two years.
15 Complete the sequence:
   see/saw/seen; wear/wore/worn; speak/........../...........
16 Give the correct forms of the verbs in brackets:
   If you (go) out now, you (get) .... wet.
17 Make a sentence with *as soon as*.
18 Which is correct? If I   **a** *win*   **b** *will win*   a lot of money, I'll buy a car.
19 Make a question with *while*.
20 Which is correct? As soon as he   **a** *will arrive*   **b** *has arrived*   he'll phone
   his wife.

Games like *Meridian Trail* can be used to animate a class and as a
form of relaxation from the usual activities of language learning.

Task: Decide if you would use a game like this in class. What
problems can you anticipate? How could you overcome them?

Other games that can be used in the classroom to practise grammar
are bingo (where a teacher reads out sentences and the students
have to identify them on a board), twenty questions (where students
ask yes/no questions to try to identify an object) and board games
(where students have to say whether the sentences they find on
certain squares are grammatically correct or not).

Written practice

Grammar practice is often done through writing. Students are
frequently given homework exercises which ask them to practise
specific language items. The following examples show some of the
more common exercise types that can be used. They start with the
most controlled kind of writing practice and end with something
that is a bit freer – even though it is still designed for the practice
of a specific grammatical item.

> **Task:** Decide which of the following two types of written practice you prefer, and why.

Fill-ins

The fill-in is a favourite technique for practising and testing writing. The students read sentences with blanks. They have to fill the blanks with specific words.

In this example for complete beginners, students are practising the difference between *is* and *are*.

> Put *is* or *are* in the blanks.
> 1 Peter _____ a doctor.
> 2 His sister Margaret _____ a reporter.
> 3 They _____ 26 years old.
> 4 Margaret and Peter _____ not twins.
> 5 Peter _____ in Turkey now. He _____ on holiday.

Fill-ins are fairly easy to write and are useful for quick practice of specific language points. Students can do them in class or as homework.

Written drills

In the following written drill for upper intermediate students from *Meanings into Words*, students have to respond to a prompt using a particular grammatical construction.

> **2 IDENTIFYING WITH 'LIKE'**
>
> Continue the following remarks with **look, sound, smell, feel or taste,** + **like.**
>
> 1 Surely he's not a manual worker...
>   *He looks like a businessman to me.*
>
> 2 Are you sure this is tea?...
>
> 3 I wonder who wrote that music...
>
> 4 He's got a foreign accent...
>
> 5 This material's very soft...
>
> 6 What's that you're cooking?...
>
> 7 They've got very similar faces...
>
> 8 This isn't real leather, is it?...
>
> 9 I've got something in my shoe...
>
> 10 I don't think you made this cake yourself...

Word order

Word order is a problem for most non-native speakers of English. This is especially so in writing.

One way of practising correct word order is to give students jumbled sentences which they then have to rearrange in the correct order. Here are some examples:

1 Ankara / on holiday. / but / lives / right now / Peter / in London / he is / in
2 at / gets / Margaret / home / half past six. / usually
3 Peter / he is / the hospital / works / in / a surgeon. / where

A way of making this activity even more involving is to put the words and phrases on large cards. Each student gets a card and they then have to rearrange themselves physically.

> **Task:** Some sections in this exercise have single words and others have more than one. Is there any reason for this, do you think?

Sentence writing

In this exercise for beginners, students are asked to write sentences about a picture using a particular verb tense. This example uses the present continuous.

Write four sentences about the picture. Say what the people are doing.

1 _____

2 _____

3 _____

4 _____

Task: If you were correcting this activity, would you yourself write out the correct version of sentences that students get wrong or would you get the students to try to do it? Why?

Parallel writing

Task: Read the postcard in the example. What language (apart from the present continuous) is being practised?

In this example for (American English) beginners from *Coast to Coast 1*, students are again being asked to practise the present continuous (amongst other things). When they have read Joan's postcard, they have to write a similar one of their own.

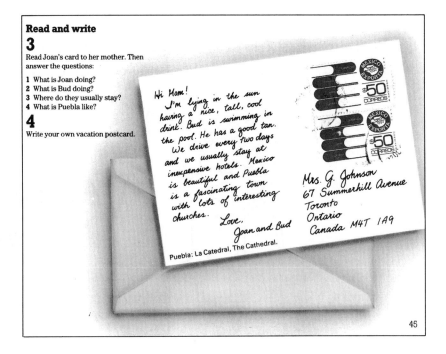

Read and write

3

Read Joan's card to her mother. Then answer the questions:

1 What is Joan doing?
2 What is Bud doing?
3 Where do they usually stay?
4 What is Puebla like?

4

Write your own vacation postcard.

Hi Mom!
I'm lying in the sun having a nice, tall, cool drink. Bud is swimming in the pool. He has a good tan. We drive every two days and we usually stay at inexpensive hotels. Mexico is beautiful and Puebla is a fascinating town with lots of interesting churches.
Love,
Joan and Bud

Mrs. G. Johnson
67 Summerhill Avenue
Toronto
Ontario
Canada M4T 1A9

Puebla: La Catedral, The Cathedral.

45

Conclusion

In this chapter we have looked at a variety of practice activities which ask students to practise certain grammatical items. Generally, the activities are designed so that the students practise the language while at the same time being involved in an enjoyable activity.

Students need to practise their grammar a lot. Where possible this will be done in pairs using interaction activities and so on. Where drills are used, the teacher must always remember that they are only a means to an end. As soon as possible they should be abandoned in favour of one of the more creative activities that we have shown in this chapter.

Exercises

1 Design an information gap activity like the one on page 44 to practise the patterns *who is he?/where does he live?/what does he do?/what's he doing right now?*
2 Write ten general knowledge questions that you think would be appropriate for your students.
3 Choose a specific language point and write a fill-in exercise to practise it.
4 Write a short text for beginner students to use as a parallel writing activity.

References

The textbook examples in this chapter have come from the following books:
Meanings into Words: Intermediate Students' Book by Adrian Doff, Christopher Jones and Keith Mitchell, p 54 (Cambridge University Press 1983)
Coast to Coast Student's Book 1 by Jeremy Harmer and Harold Surguine, p 74 (Longman 1987)
Caring and Sharing in the Foreign Language Class by Gertrude Moskowitz, p 120 (Newbury House 1978)

Meridian Activity Book 2 by Jeremy Harmer and Steve Elsworth, pp 34, 74, 75 (Longman 1986)
Meanings into Words: Upper Intermediate. Workbook by Adrian Doff, Christopher Jones and Keith Mitchell, p 10 (Cambridge University Press 1984)
Coast to Coast Student's Book 1 p 45

Acknowledgement

1 I first saw the 'crimes' drill (p 46) used by Mario Rinvolucri.

Testing grammar

In this chapter we are going to look at how to test the students' knowledge of grammar. We will look at a number of types of test items.

Types of test

We can test the students' ability to speak or write. We can test students' reading or listening comprehension skills. Many tests include all these elements, especially public exams like those from the University of Cambridge or the Oxford Delegacy, for example, which have four or five separate papers. But because marking written tests is easier than marking oral tests – and because written tests take less time and are easier to administer – most tests are based on the written skills, especially when they are designed for individual schools and colleges. Many teachers feel that this is unsatisfactory since so much teaching in the classroom is based on oral work, but as yet no one has come up with a practical solution to the problems of time and administration with oral tests for large numbers of students.

Public exams test how good a student's overall command of English is. In this chapter, however, we will look at tests which are given in schools and classes to find out how well students have done. These are often called *achievement* tests and are given after four or six weeks' study, or after three or four units of a coursebook, or after a semester or year's work. The aim of such tests is to see if students have learnt and acquired the language they have been studying or have been exposed to. Tests are usually written by heads of departments or by teachers of individual classes.

Writing achievement tests

Writing a test is an important job that demands skill and patience. Good tests show both teacher and students how well they are all doing. They do not fail students unnecessarily and they give everyone a chance to show how much they have learnt.

Tests can often go wrong, not just because of the students' lack of knowledge, but also because of problems in the writing of the tests themselves. When writing tests teachers should bear in mind the following five 'rules'.

1 Don't test what you haven't taught

The purpose of an achievement test is to find out how well students have achieved what they have been studying. In such a test, then, it is not fair to test things that they haven't been exposed to. Stick to the language that you have been studying unless you are testing reading or listening comprehension (where the students' ability to understand unfamiliar words is one of the things you will be looking at). Of course, where students are being asked to write freely, they can be encouraged to be as ambitious as you want them to be (see 4 below).

2 Don't test general knowledge

Test writers should remember that they are testing the students' knowledge of *English*, not their knowledge of the world. For example, a test item like this would not be acceptable.

Picasso was a famous _____.

It is, after all, quite possible that your students have never heard of Picasso, especially if they are young or come from non-European cultures. The problem is that if students get this item wrong, you don't know if it is because they don't know about Picasso or because they don't know the word *painter* (or *artist*).

3 Don't introduce new techniques in tests

One thing that confuses students in tests, is the presence of item types and techniques that they have never seen before. In other words, if students are given a set of jumbled words and asked to reorder them to make a sentence, we would expect them to have seen this type of activity before in class. If the sentence-ordering activity is completely new to them, they may have difficulties understanding how to do the question which have nothing to do with their knowledge of English (or lack of it).

4 Don't just test accuracy

Although we will be looking mainly at items which test grammatical accuracy in this chapter, it is vital that an achievement test examines the students' ability to use language, not just their knowledge of grammatical accuracy. In other words students must be given a chance to write a letter, a description or an essay (for example) at some stage in the test. The teacher marking the test can then see if the students are able to express themselves freely, as well as being able to do questions about specific language items. Items which only test one thing (e.g. a verb form or a question word) have been called *discrete* items. Test items which test the students' whole knowledge of the language – like essay writing – have been called *integrative*.

5 Don't forget to test the test

It is extremely unwise to write a test and give it straight to the students. Often unforeseen problems arise. Perhaps you forgot to write clear instructions. Perhaps there are some mistakes. Perhaps the test is far too difficult – or far too easy. But especially if the test is important for students (and most tests are) you must try to ensure that it works.

The first thing to do when you have just written a test is to show it to colleagues. They will often spot problems that you have not thought of – and they may be able to suggest improvements. At the very least they should spot misprints! If possible you should try your test out with a class of students similar to your own. Sometimes the best way to do this is to get a class of a slightly higher level than your own to try it out. If they can do it fairly comfortably then you've probably got the level about right.

But even if you can't try out your test on other students, you must get other people to read it to spot any obvious mistakes or problems.

Test items

We can now look at a number of items that test a student's

knowledge of grammar. We will start by looking at more *discrete* items (see 4 above) and end by looking at testing techniques that are slightly more *integrative*.

> **Task:** For each of the following test types find out a) exactly what the exercise is testing, b) how you would mark it, c) how easy it would be for your students, and d) how much of a test with fifty marks you would devote to this kind of test.

Multiple choice

In multiple choice items, students have to choose the correct answer from a number of alternatives. At the most simple level, multiple choice can be used to test the students' grammatical knowledge, for example:

Choose the correct answer, a, b, c or d.

1 Charles _____ to work yesterday.
   a) doesn't go b) hasn't gone c) didn't go d) isn't going

2 Charles is going _____ his grandmother tomorrow.
   a) visit b) to visit c) visiting d) visited

3 I want to buy _____ new furniture.
   a) some b) a c) two d) something

Multiple choice items can be made a greater test of all-round comprehension if they are part of a passage or dialogue, for example:

HILARY: Where are you a) on   to?
                      b) in
                      c) off
                      d) out
JANE: I'm just going to the shops.
HILARY: Could you a) post   this letter with you?
                  b) take
                  c) bring
                  d) buy
JANE: Yes, of course.
HILARY: And you'd better a) take   an umbrella.
                         b) to take
                         c) taking
                         d) took
JANE: Why?
HILARY: Because it's going to rain.

Multiple choice items like this have the great advantage of being easy to mark. But it is difficult to write 'distractors' (the three wrong answers), which aren't either absurd – or possible – as well as the correct answer. Special care should be taken to make sure that there is only one correct answer.

Multiple choice items like this test the students' recognition of grammatical items. They are not tests of the students' productive ability.

Fill-ins

Fill-ins are those items where students have to fill a blank with a word or words. Often students see five separate sentences and have to fill in a word for each. In this example from the tests of *Opening Strategies* (at beginner level) however, the students have to understand a whole text at the same time and then write the words on a separate sheet of paper.

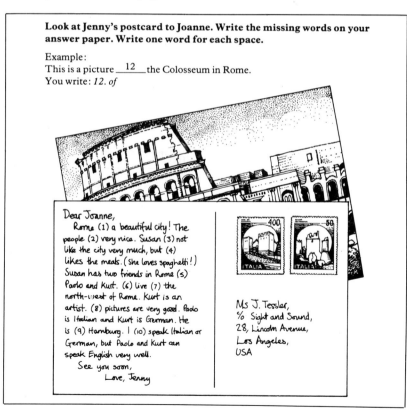

Look at Jenny's postcard to Joanne. Write the missing words on your answer paper. Write one word for each space.

Example:
This is a picture ___12___ the Colosseum in Rome.
You write: *12. of*

Dear Joanne,
   Rome (1) a beautiful city! The people (2) very nice. Susan (3) not like the city very much, but (4) likes the meals. (She loves spaghetti!) Susan has two friends in Rome (5) Paolo and Kurt. (6) live (7) the north-west of Rome. Kurt is an artist. (8) pictures are very good. Paolo is Italian and Kurt is German. He is (9) Hamburg. I (10) speak Italian or German, but Paolo and Kurt can speak English very well.
      See you soon,
         Love, Jenny

Ms J. Tessler,
% Sight and Sound,
28, Lincoln Avenue,
Los Angeles,
USA

This is a good test of students' comprehension as well as of their knowledge of individual grammatical items (such as personal pronouns, prepositions, and the verb *to be*, etc). It is certainly more integrative than the traditional fill-in item such as *He ate _____ orange after lunch.*

Fill-in items are easy to write, although it is sometimes difficult to ensure that students can put in only one answer! Even in our *orange* example, readers will be able to come up with more than one word to put in the blank which could be correct. Test writers will have to try their best to write items which only allow one answer, but they should be prepared to accept other correct possibilities that they had not previously thought of.

Sentence completion

Fill-in items usually ask for only one word. But they can be extended to test more of the students' knowledge and use of English. Students have to fill in a blank and/or complete a sentence with more than one word. There will often be more than one way of doing this. Test items like this are usually called sentence completions.

In this example from a progress test from *Meanings into Words* (at the upper intermediate level), students have to choose language that 'makes sense'.

---

3   GAP-FILLING   *4 marks*

Complete the sentences below so that they make sense.

1 A: Are you sure you'll be all right?
   B: Don't worry – I'm .... looking after myself.
2 Both teams were exhausted. They .... for three hours.
3 The old lady, who .... , suddenly sat up and asked for some tea.
4 He was born between 1940 and 1942, so he must be in ....

Obviously students who complete this task successfully show that they have a lot of grammatical knowledge and that they are able to use the right vocabulary and grammar to complete the task. In that sense these are quite integrative tasks. But they will be difficult to mark accurately. Do students get extra marks for trying to be more 'advanced'? Do all mistakes lose the same amount of marks? Obviously the writers of this test do not have only one correct answer in mind, but deciding what to accept makes the test marker's task quite complex.

Sentence reordering

If students are used to this activity, then part of a test (for beginners) might look like this:

Put the words in order to make correct sentences.

1 he lives / John is / and / in London. / a student

_____

2 a housewife and / is / His sister / she is / secretary. / a

_____

3 at home now, / isn't / in Canada. / His sister / she is

_____

4 Thursday. / Toronto / She was / on / in

_____

5 on holiday in / in London, / John / he is / France. / isn't

_____

This type of test item explores the students' knowledge of syntax and is a useful addition to a test. However it should not be confused with a test of production and once again test writers must be sure that if more than one order is possible (and it often is) all possible orders should be marked as correct.

Transformations

A test of the students' knowledge of syntax and structure is sentence transformation. Here students have to rewrite sentences so that they have the same meaning but different grammatical structure. Here are some examples:

Complete the sentences so that they mean the same as the original sentence. Start with the words given.
1 John is taller than Mary.

Mary isn't _____

2 'I haven't seen her for years', he said.

He said that —————————————————————

3 I won't come unless you ring.

I'll come —————————————————————

4 She wasn't strong enough to lift the suitcase.

The suitcase —————————————————————

Once again, this is the kind of test type that students need to be prepared for. Students should have practised transforming sentences before they come across this exercise. But the ability to transform sentences correctly certainly implies quite a lot of grammatical knowledge – although it may take a certain kind of 'intelligence' to be very good at it.

Sentence writing

As we saw in chapter five, students can practise their sentence writing by describing a picture, as in this example:

Write four sentences about this picture using *there is* and *there are*.

1 —————————————————————

2 —————————————————————

3 —————————————————————

4 —————————————————————

This activity certainly tests the students' ability to write correct sentences – and their ability to use *there* with *is* and *are* correctly. It is not, of course, a very creative exercise, and, although more integrative than a single sentence fill-in, does not really test language use.

Parallel writing

One way of providing a fairly controlled integrative test type is through parallel writing. Here you ask the students to use their knowledge of grammar and vocabulary to imitate a piece they have read (and understood). The following example from a test for *Track 2* (at the elementary level) shows the technique in practice.

G Writing (10 marks)

Read this passage, and look at the map.

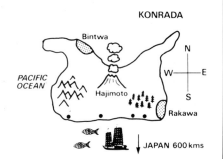

The island of Konrada is in the Pacific Ocean, 600 kilometres north of Japan. There are a lot of mountains in the west of the island and a big forest in the south east. There is a big volcano in the middle of the island. The name of the volcano is 'Hajimoto'.

There are two big cities. Bintwa is in the north and Rakawa is in the south east. Most of the people live in the cities. A few people live near the sea in the south of the island. These people are fishermen.

Now write about the island of Binat. Use these notes and look at the map.

island / Binat / Atlantic Ocean / 300 kilometres / west / Africa. // mountains / north / island. // big forest / south west. // big volcano / middle / island. // name / volcano / Fire Mountain. // two big cities. // Crofta / south east / and / Portland / west. // most / people / live / cities. // few people / near / volcano / middle / island. // people / farmers. //

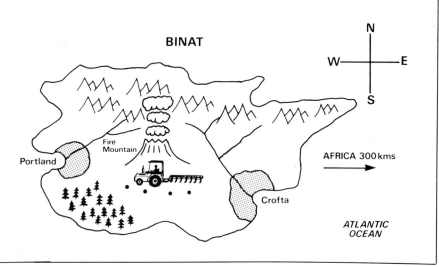

The students are given notes to help them write their own paragraph, and this may be especially helpful since this material is designed for young teenagers. The activity would be even more challenging, of course, if the notes were not there.

Parallel writing is quite a good compromise between discrete and integrative test types. The test writer can include the grammar he wants students to produce in the original paragraph and hope that the students will reuse it in their own piece of writing. The test writer can make the original paragraph more or less controlled.

In order to complete this task successfully, students need to understand a paragraph, its form and its grammar. Once again, the test writer should be sure that students have previously used this technique in class since it might otherwise cause confusion.

Conclusion

In this chapter we have looked at a number of exercises which test grammar, together with some 'rules' or hints about test design.

We have stressed the need for test exercises which encourage the students' written production as well as items which concentrate on accuracy. Most of our examples have been of the latter kind, but we should not forget activities like essays, compositions, and letter writing. As soon as students start using language in this way, though, grammar is just *one* of the things which is being tested – and that is why such exercises have not been included in this book.

Exercises

1 Write some multiple choice items to test the students' knowledge of the difference between simple and continuous verbs (present, present perfect past and past perfect tenses).
2 Write a five item sentence-completion exercise for a final test at the lower intermediate level. Try to make all the items refer to the same context.
3 Write three transformation items to test either reported speech or the second conditional or *so/such a . . . that . . .* Look at the

parallel writing test item above. How would you mark this item? How many marks do students lose for mistakes? Are all spelling mistakes going to be penalised? What does a student need to do to score full marks on this exercise?

References

The textbook examples in this chapter have come from the following publications:
Opening Strategies Tests by Nick Dawson, p 5 (Longman 1983)
Meanings into Words: Upper Intermediate. Test Book by Adrian Doff, Christopher Jones and Keith Mitchell, p 6 (Cambridge University Press 1984)
Track Tests 1 2 3 by Nick Dawson, p 26 (Longman 1985)

Final task

Say whether you agree with these statements by scoring them from 0 (if you completely disagree) to 5 (if you completely agree).

1 All grammar teaching should be covert. Teachers should not draw students' attention to grammatical facts and rules.   0 1 2 3 4 5

2 Students should discover facts about grammar through problem-solving activities. Teachers should not teach such facts.   0 1 2 3 4 5

3 The best kind of grammar practice is written grammar practice.   0 1 2 3 4 5

4 The only language that you can really test with any accuracy is grammar.   0 1 2 3 4 5

5 Children do not learn grammar rules when they acquire their first language, so adults don't need to either.   0 1 2 3 4 5

Compare your results for this task with your results for the first task of chapter one. Have your opinions altered as you have read the book?

Suggestions for further reading

There are many books about grammar available nowadays, and many more collections of grammar exercises continue to be produced. A list of all the books which have been published would be extremely long: for that reason we will list only a few titles from amongst the many excellent books in the shops. We will look at two kinds of books; books about grammar and grammar practice books.

Books about grammar

BALD, W, COBB, D AND SCHWARZ, A *Active Grammar* (Longman 1986)
This is a simple reference grammar which describes the structures and forms encountered at basic and elementary levels. It is clearly laid out and it is accompanied by examples. It includes cartoons. There is an accompanying book of exercises.

BOLITHO, R AND TOMLINSON, B *Discover English* (Heinemann 1980)
The authors called this a 'language awareness' book and it was developed for use with advanced students and trainee teachers. Readers are made aware of problems and usages in English grammar through 'discovery techniques' (see chapter four). In the second half of the book the authors provide solutions to the problems they have set.

SHEPHERD, J, ROSSNER, R AND TAYLOR, J *Ways to Grammar* (Macmillan 1984)
This is a grammar practice book intended for intermediate students. However, each section is prefaced by a description of the points to be dealt with and there are extremely useful summary charts which lay grammatical information out in a sensible way. While not being as comprehensive as *Practical English Usage*, (see below) there is a lot of clear explanation here.

SWAN, M *Basic English Usage* (Oxford University Press 1984)
This book concentrates on the most recurrent problems in English usage. It is arranged alphabetically and shows typical mistakes together with correct forms and usage. There is an accompanying book of exercises.

SWAN, M *Practical English Usage* (Oxford University Press 1980)
This is the more advanced version of *Basic English Usage*. It is
designed for upper intermediate and advanced students, but many
teachers have also found it useful as a reference guide.
Grammatical points are arranged alphabetically and common
mistakes are mentioned. The language of the explanations is clear
and accessible and the number of entries and the points covered is
extremely comprehensive.

Serious students of English will also want to consult these two
titles:

QUIRK, R, GREENBAUM, S, LEECH, G and SVARTVIK, J *A
Comprehensive Grammar of the English Language* (Longman 1985)
This is the most complete and authoritative grammar of the English
language for both native and non-native speakers of English
grammar.

QUIRK, R and GREENBAUM, S *A University Grammar of English*
(Longman 1973)
This concentrates on present-day English grammar and makes
distinctions between spoken and written, formal and informal,
American and British, usage.

Grammar practice books

Apart from the exercises which accompany the books about
grammar and the practice material in *Ways to Grammar*, here are
some other practice titles:

ELSWORTH, S AND WALKER, E *Grammar Practice for Intermediate
Students* (Longman 1986)
This collection of exercises is for students at an intermediate level
(or above). The grammar is clearly explained and then students do a
variety of exercises which are often accompanied by humorous
cartoons.

GRAVER, B D *Advanced English Practice* (New Edition) (Oxford
University Press 1985)
This favourite for teachers of advanced students has exercises on a
great variety of grammar points in the English language. Much of
the language is at a very advanced level. Some of the exercises are
a bit out-of-date, but this is a solid collection of practice activities
for students at this level.

HIGGINS, M *Elementary Grammar Workbooks 1, 2 and 3* (Longman 1985)
These three workbooks cover the grammar found at the elementary level. Students write in the books for the various exercise types. Each section is preceded by a chart which lays out the point(s) to be practised.

MURPHY, R *English Grammar in Use* (Cambridge University Press 1985)
This is for intermediate and advanced students. Grammar explanations with exercises are provided, and there is a detailed index and appendices dealing with tenses, spelling, etc.

SEIDL, J *Grammar in Practice 1 and 2* (Oxford University Press 1982)
Grammar points at the elementary level are presented through a series of dialogues and texts and then practised in a variety of exercises.